ESSENTIAL TECHNIQUE FOR STRINGS

An Essential Elements Method

INTERMEDIATE TECHNIQUE STUDIES

Flexible Sequence Format

Choose pages from the 3 major sections:

- I. Higher Positions and Shifting
- II. Keys and Scales
- III. Bowings and Special Techniques

Essential Technique For Strings is a book of studies to help the intermediate player develop the skills necessary for playing in an orchestra. Chronologically, it follows Book 2 of *Essential Elements For Strings*, but is designed as a multi-use technique book for use within a string orchestra setting. It is organized so that you can use the various sections in the book in the way that's best for your individual needs.

By

Michael Allen • Robert Gillespie • Pamela Tellejohn Hayes

ISBN 978-0-7935-7149-9

HAL•LEONARD®
CORPORATION

7777 W. BLUEMOUND RD. P.O. BOX 13819 MILWAUKEE, WI 53213

POSITIONS

D STRING

3RD ½ POSITION

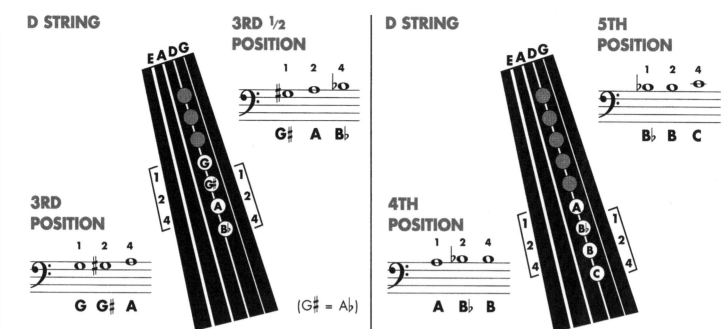

G♯   A   B♭

3RD POSITION

G   G♯   A

(G♯ = A♭)

D STRING

5TH POSITION

B♭   B   C

4TH POSITION

A   B♭   B

1.

2.

3.

4.

5.

6.

G STRING

5TH POSITION

4TH POSITION

G STRING

5TH ½ POSITION

HARMONIC

POSITIONS

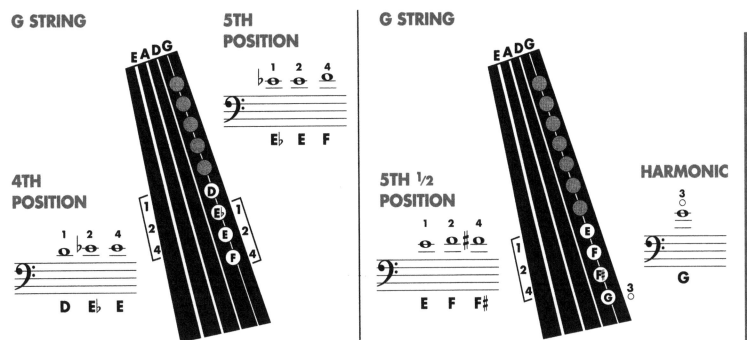

7.

8.

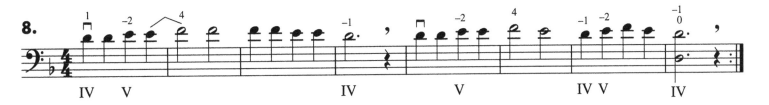

9.

10.

$\overset{3}{\underset{o}{}}$ = HARMONIC (see page 5).

11.

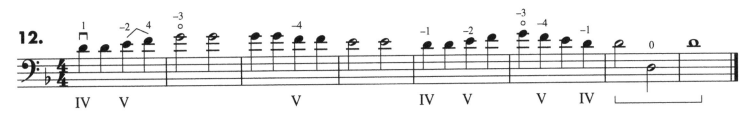

12.

G STRING

3RD POSITION

The **symphony** has its roots in late 18th century central Europe. The Classical Austro/German composer, Haydn, wrote over one hundred symphonies and is credited with setting a standard of symphonic composition that was a model for those who followed. Haydn's contemporary, Mozart, added to the symphony by expanding melodic content as well as form. Beethoven brought the symphony into the Romantic age by expanding form further as well as changing instrumentation. Following Beethoven were numerous Romantic composers such as Tchaikovsky, Brahms and Dvorak who developed harmony, rhythm and folk elements. By the late 1800's, Mahler's and Bruckner's compositions were so developed that they hardly resembled the symphonies of Haydn.

18. SYMPHONY NO. 1 THEME

Gustav Mahler

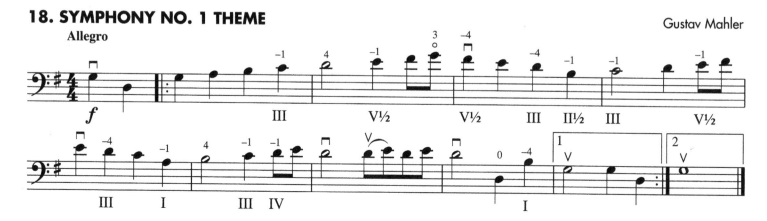

Theory

Natural Harmonic Natural harmonics are tones created by a vibrating string divided into equal sections. To play an octave higher than an open string, lightly touch the string exactly half way between the bridge and the nut. Harmonics are indicated by a "°" above a note and below a fingering number: 3̥ indicates a harmonic played with the third finger.

POSITIONS

27.

28.

29.

30.

31.

32.

33.

34.

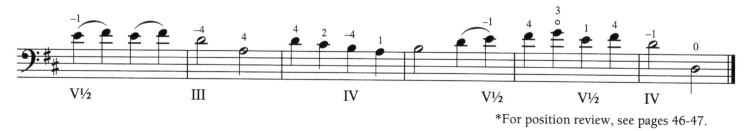

*For position review, see pages 46-47.

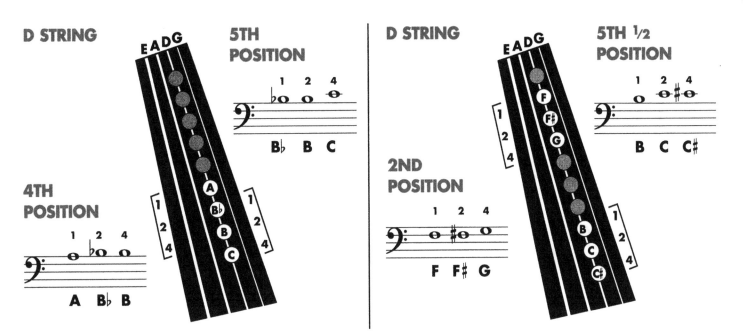

D STRING

5TH POSITION

4TH POSITION

D STRING

5TH ½ POSITION

2ND POSITION

35.

36.

37.

38.

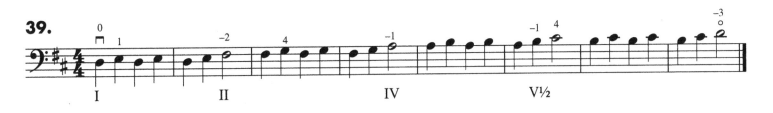

39.

40.

History

Folk songs are any songs of unknown authorship which have been passed down from generation to generation. Some folk songs come from specific ethnic groups or nationalities such as this song from France. Others are associated with a certain profession or even a specific family. Sea chanteys and some Christmas carols could be thought of as folk songs. Many composers quote folk songs in their compositions.

41. FRENCH FOLK SONG

42. CAN CAN

Jacques Offenbach

43.

44.

45.

46.

47.

48.

49.

50.

51.

52.

POSITIONS

9

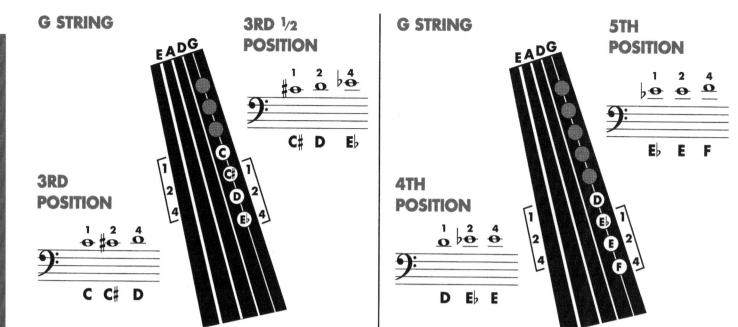

G STRING

3RD POSITION

C C# D

3RD ½ POSITION

C# D Eb

G STRING

4TH POSITION

D Eb E

5TH POSITION

Eb E F

53.

III

54.

III   III½   III   III½   III III½   III

55.

III   IV   III   IV   III IV   III

56.

III   IV   III IV   III   III½   III III½   III

57.

III   V   III   V   III

58.

III   V   III   V   III

G STRING

2ND POSITION

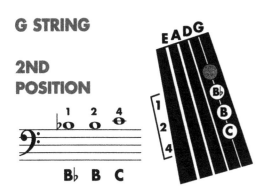

B♭ B C

59.

Time Signature (Meter)

6 - 6 beats per measure
8 - ♪ or 𝄾 gets one beat (slower music)

♪	= 1 beat
♩	= 2 beats
♩.	= 3 beats
♩.	= 6 beats

When music is slow, **6/8** time should be counted 6 beats to a measure with the eighth note receiving 1 beat. Place a slight accent on beats 1 and 4 when tapping and counting aloud.

60. ROW, ROW, ROW YOUR BOAT - Round

61. LONG, LONG AGO

62. MICHAEL ROW YOUR BOAT ASHORE

63. BLUE BELLS OF SCOTLAND

D.S. al Fine Play until you see the *D.S. al Fine*, then go back to the sign (𝄋) and play until you see the word *Fine* (finish). D.S. is the Italian abbreviation for *Dal segno*, "from the sign."

70. HOME ON THE RANGE

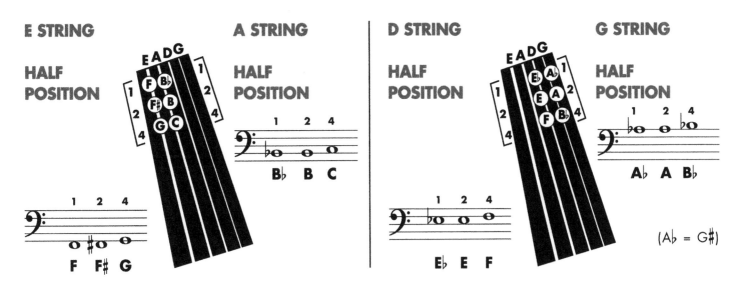

E STRING

HALF POSITION

F F♯ G

A STRING

HALF POSITION

B♭ B C

D STRING

HALF POSITION

E♭ E F

G STRING

HALF POSITION

A♭ A B♭

(A♭ = G♯)

71.

72.

73.

74.

75.

76.

POSITIONS

D STRING

2ND POSITION

2ND ½ POSITION

D STRING

3RD POSITION

4TH POSITION

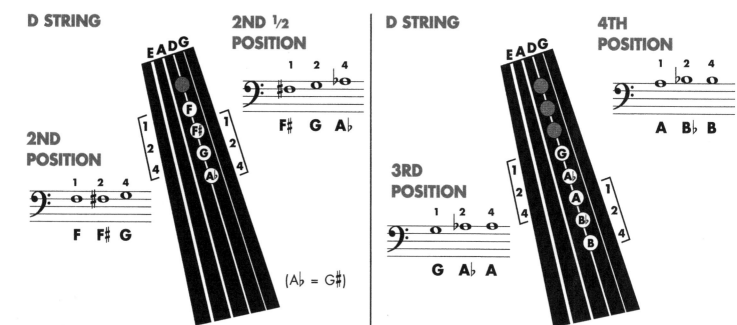

(A♭ = G♯)

77.

78.

79.

80.

81.

82.

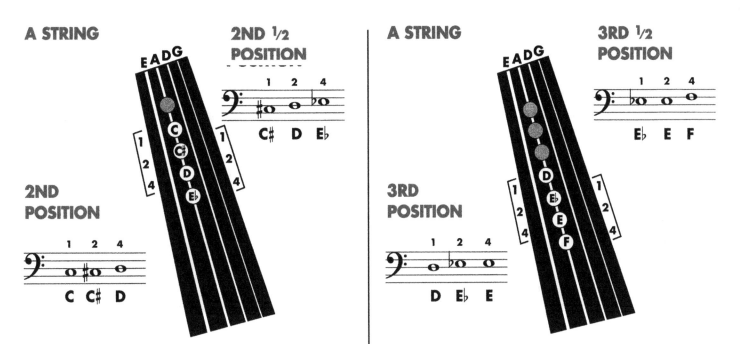

POSITIONS

83.

84.

85.

86.

87.

88.

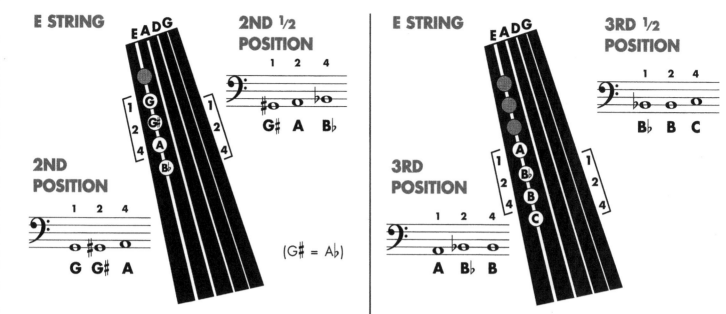

E STRING

2ND ½ POSITION

1 2 4

G# A B♭

2ND POSITION

1 2 4

G G# A

(G# = A♭)

E STRING

3RD ½ POSITION

1 2 4

B♭ B C

3RD POSITION

1 2 4

A B♭ B

89.

90.

91.

92.

93.

94.

95.

96.

97.

98.

99. THE FIRST NOEL

FOR BASSES ONLY

Write the finger number underneath each note in the following lines.

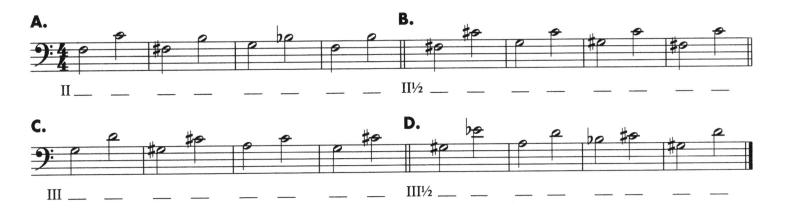

A.

II __ __ __ __ __ __ __

B.

II½ __ __ __ __ __ __ __

C.

III __ __ __ __ __ __ __

D.

III½ __ __ __ __ __ __ __

C MAJOR

100. FINGER PATTERNS IN C MAJOR

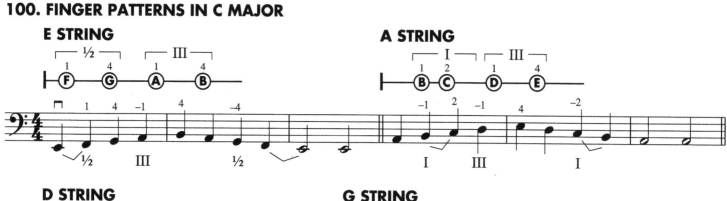

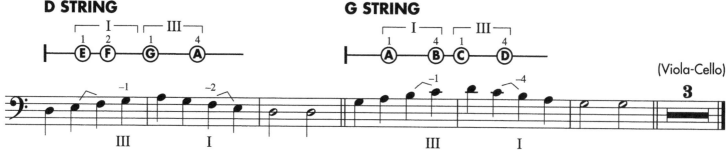

101. C MAJOR SCALE

102. C MAJOR ARPEGGIO

103. THIRDS IN C MAJOR

MAJOR KEYS

104. THE BRITISH GRENADIERS

Allegro

Johann Sebastian Bach (1685-1750) is probably best remembered as an organist and church musician, but he also wrote hundreds of compositions for the royal courts of Germany and Austria. For example, *The Brandenburg Concertos* are six works for instrumental ensembles dedicated to the court at Brandenburg. Bach lived at the same time the original thirteen colonies were being settled by European immigrants.

105. CHORALE IN C

A = Melody. **B** = Harmony (orchestra part).

J.S. Bach

MAJOR KEYS

G MAJOR

106. FINGER PATTERNS IN G MAJOR

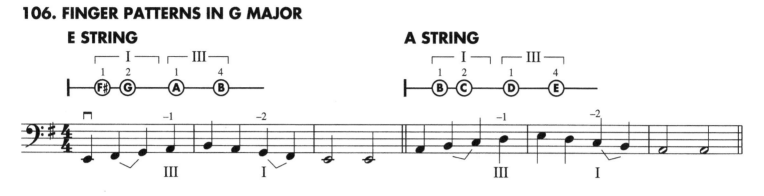

E STRING

A STRING

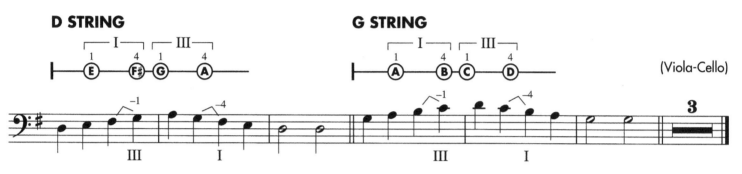

D STRING

G STRING

(Viola-Cello)

107. G MAJOR SCALE

108. G MAJOR ARPEGGIO

109. THIRDS IN G MAJOR

110. DONA NOBIS PACEM - Canon/Round

Traditional Canon

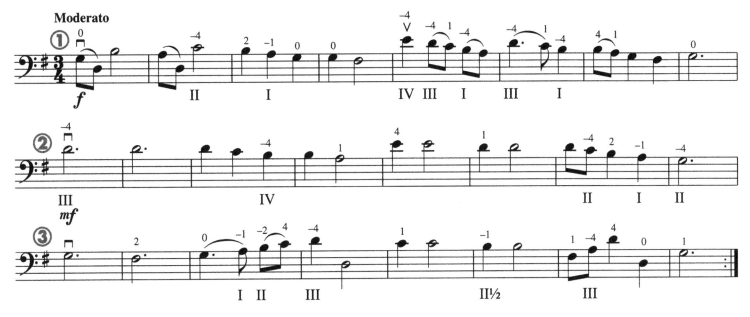

111. CHORALE IN G

A = Melody. **B** = Harmony (orchestra part).

J.S. Bach

MAJOR KEYS

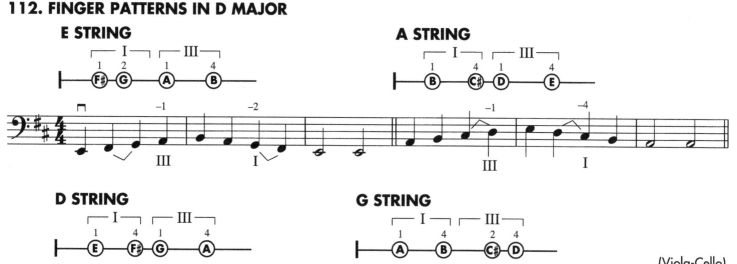

D MAJOR

112. FINGER PATTERNS IN D MAJOR

113. D MAJOR SCALE

114. D MAJOR ARPEGGIO

115. THIRDS IN D MAJOR

MAJOR KEYS

116. SHENANDOAH

American Folk Song

117. CHORALE IN D

A = Melody. **B** = Harmony (orchestra part).

J.S. Bach

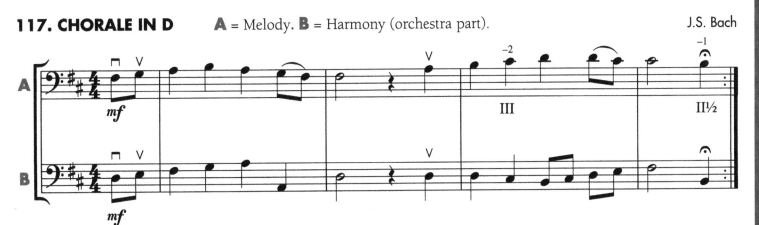

MAJOR KEYS

A MAJOR

118. FINGER PATTERNS IN A MAJOR

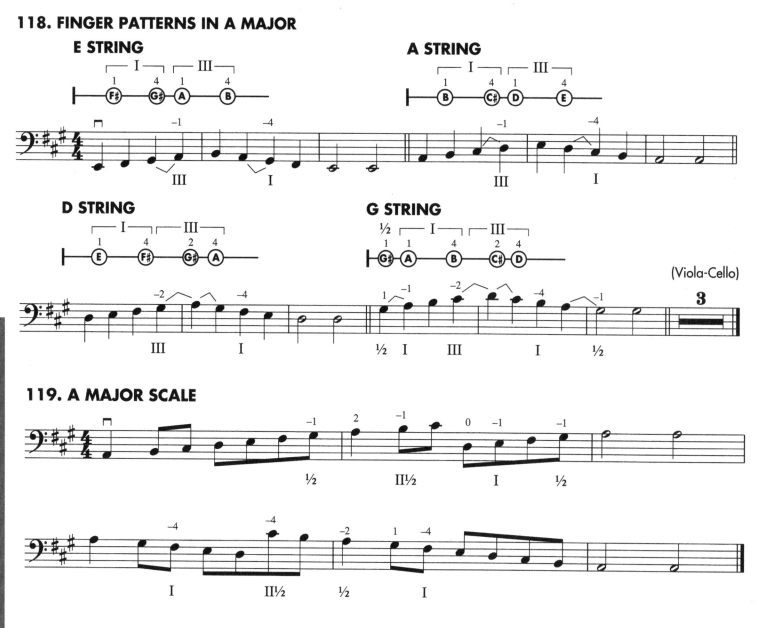

119. A MAJOR SCALE

120. A MAJOR ARPEGGIO

121. THIRDS IN A MAJOR

122. THE YELLOW ROSE OF TEXAS

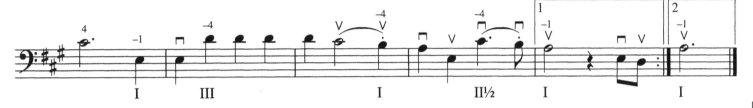

123. CHORALE IN A

A = Melody. **B** = Harmony (orchestra part).

J.S. Bach

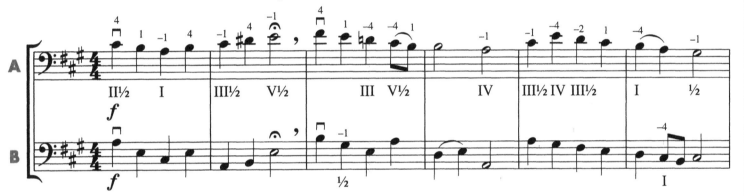

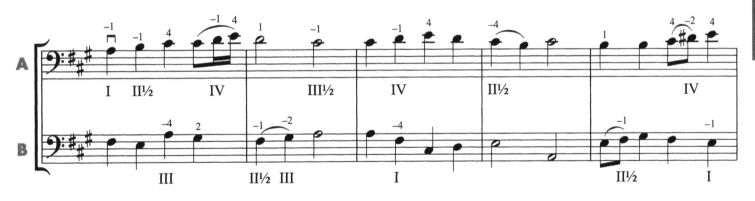

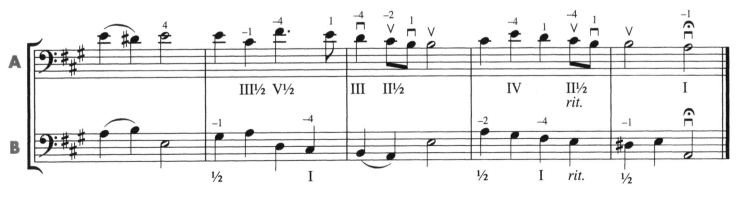

MAJOR KEYS

F MAJOR

124. FINGER PATTERNS IN F MAJOR

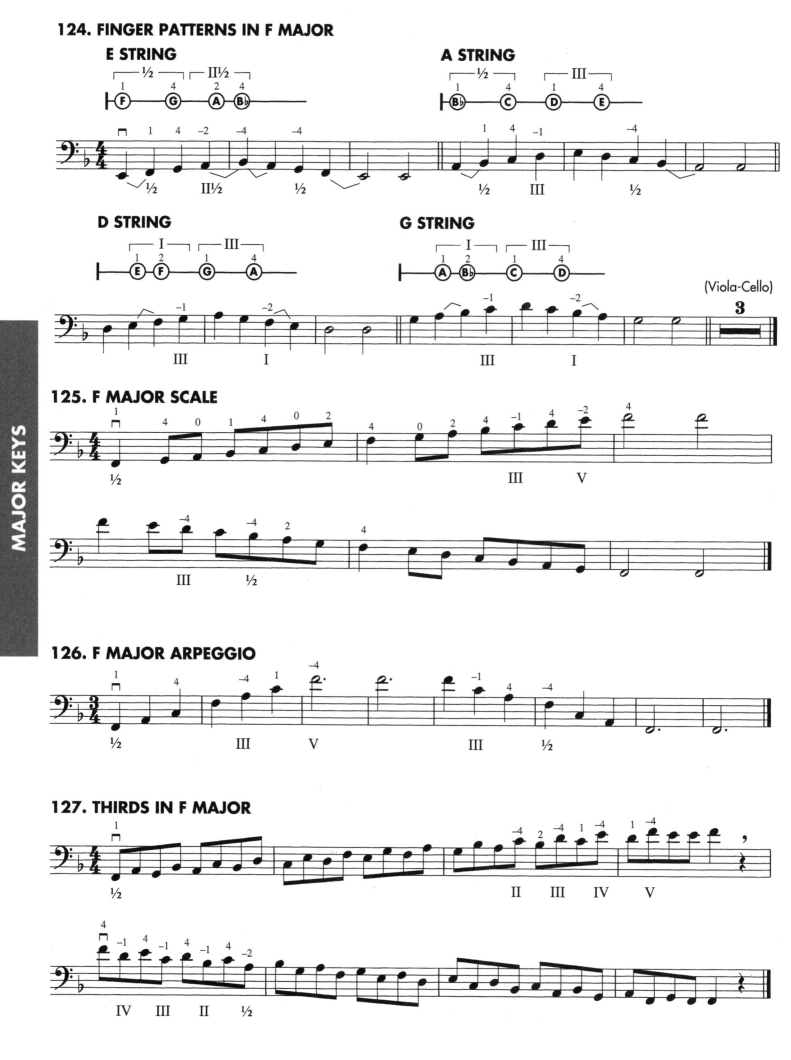

125. F MAJOR SCALE

126. F MAJOR ARPEGGIO

127. THIRDS IN F MAJOR

MAJOR KEYS

128. BELLA-BOCCA POLKA

Emil Waldteufel

Allegretto

129. CHORALE IN F

A = Melody. B = Harmony (orchestra part).

J.S. Bach

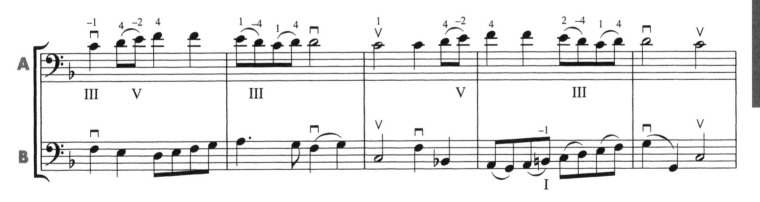

MAJOR KEYS

B♭ MAJOR

130. FINGER PATTERNS IN B♭ MAJOR

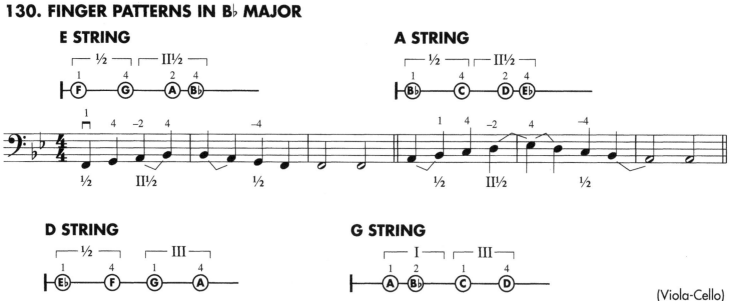

131. B♭ MAJOR SCALE

132. B♭ MAJOR ARPEGGIO

133. THIRDS IN B♭ MAJOR

MAJOR KEYS

134. JOHN PEEL

135. CHORALE IN B♭

A = Melody. **B** = Harmony (orchestra part).

J.S. Bach

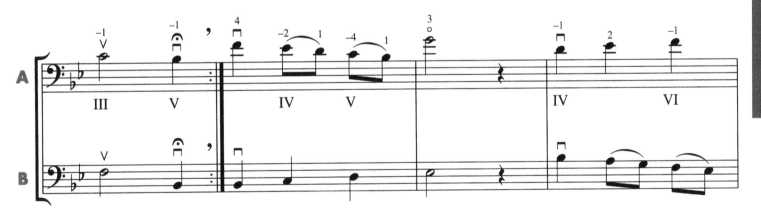

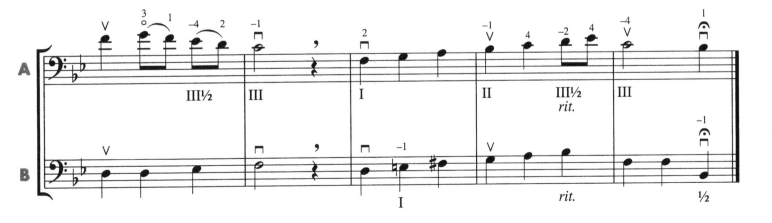

MAJOR KEYS

E♭ MAJOR

136. FINGER PATTERNS IN E♭ MAJOR

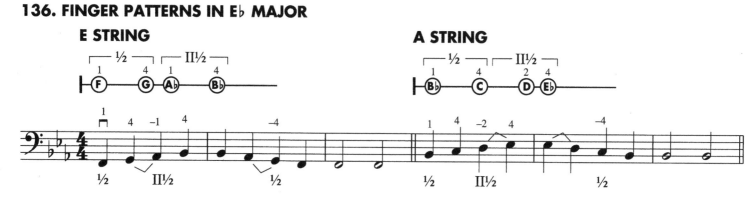

137. E♭ MAJOR SCALE

138. E♭ MAJOR ARPEGGIO

139. THIRDS IN E♭ MAJOR

MAJOR KEYS

History

German composer **Richard Wagner** (1813-1883) was one of the leaders in opera of the mid to late 1800's. He brought musical drama to a new height with elaborate sets, large orchestras, and new lengths of performance (most of his operas lasted for several hours). His goal was to create a new art form where music and drama were of equal importance. While Richard Wagner was transforming the musical and dramatic aesthetic, the rest of the modern world was changing dramatically as well. The first railroads were being built, the Americans fought a civil war, and Alexander Graham Bell invented the telephone.

140. PILGRIM'S CHORUS FROM TANNHÄUSER

Richard Wagner

Andante Maestoso

141. CHORALE IN E♭

A = Melody. **B** = Harmony (orchestra part).

J.S. Bach

MAJOR KEYS

A MINOR

142. A NATURAL MINOR

143. A HARMONIC MINOR

144. A MELODIC MINOR

145. A MINOR ARPEGGIO

146. SONG OF THE SHAKUHACHI

Japanese Folk Song

147. SCARBOROUGH FAIR

Gently

MINOR KEYS

E MINOR

148. E NATURAL MINOR

149. E HARMONIC MINOR

150. E MELODIC MINOR

151. E MINOR ARPEGGIO

152. LA CINQUANTAINE

J. Gabriel-Marie

Allegretto

153. BOURÉE FROM SUITE IN E MINOR FOR LUTE

J.S. Bach

Allegro

MINOR KEYS

D MINOR

154. D NATURAL MINOR

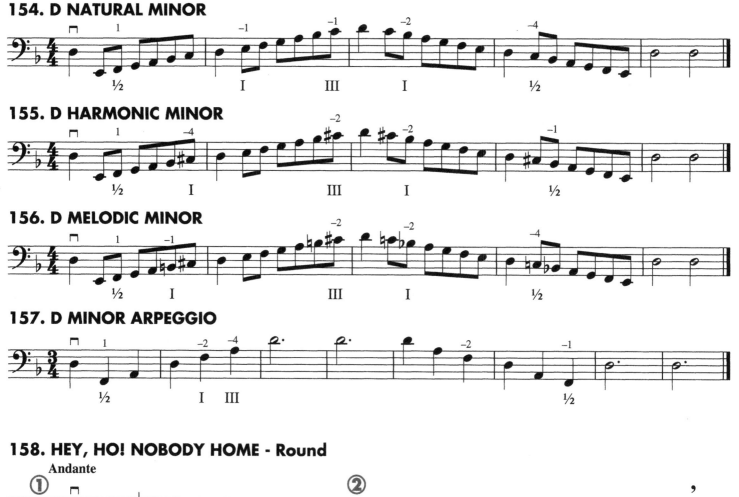

155. D HARMONIC MINOR

156. D MELODIC MINOR

157. D MINOR ARPEGGIO

158. HEY, HO! NOBODY HOME - Round

Andante

159. ZUM GALI GALI

Israeli Folk Song

Moderato

mp

mf

mp

MINOR KEYS

G MINOR

160. G NATURAL MINOR

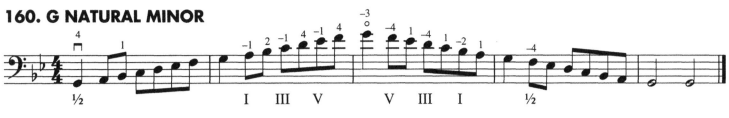

161. G HARMONIC MINOR

*See pp. 46-47 for position review.

162. G MELODIC MINOR

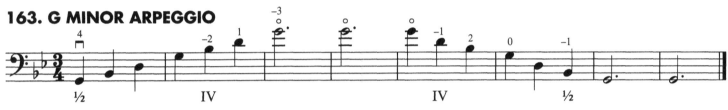

163. G MINOR ARPEGGIO

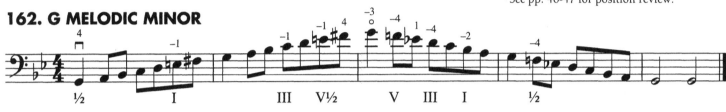

Spirituals are religious folk songs originating within the African-American community. They were originally associated with work, recreation, or religious gatherings. Spirituals remain popular today probably due to their strong rhythmic character and melodic lines.

164. JOSHUA

African-American Spiritual

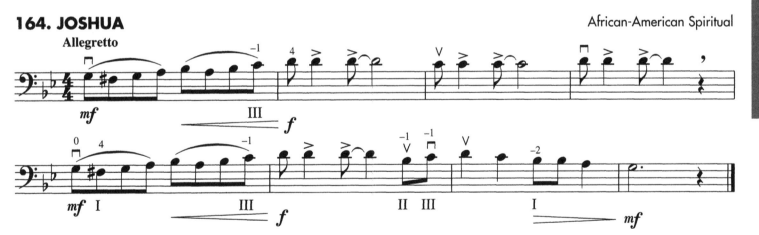

165. RUSSIAN SAILOR'S DANCE

Reinhold Glière

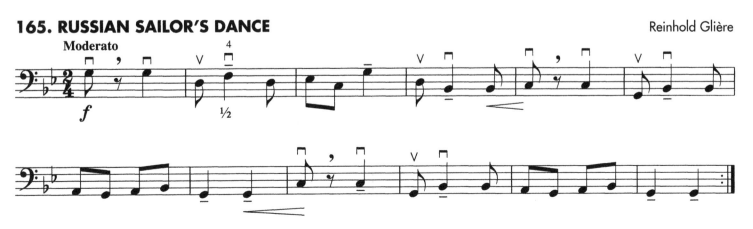

MINOR KEYS

C MINOR

166. C NATURAL MINOR

167. C HARMONIC MINOR

168. C MELODIC MINOR

169. C MINOR ARPEGGIO

 Czech composer **Bedrich Smetana** (1824-84) was one of several 19th century composers who infused native folk themes into his compositions. "Moldau," named for a river in Bohemia, is one theme that is part of a collection of songs, entitled *Má Vlast* or "my homeland." While composers of the 19th century were returning to their folk roots for inspiration, artists and writers were turning to more realistic reflections of current society. Charles Dickens was writing *David Copperfield* and *A Tale of Two Cities*, and Vincent van Gogh and Claude Monet both created images of urban and country life.

170. MOLDAU

Bedrich Smetana

Allegretto

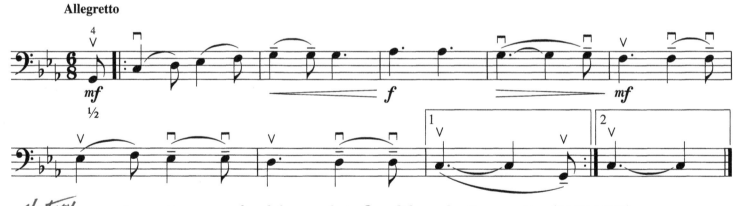

 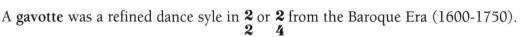 A **gavotte** was a refined dance syle in $\frac{2}{2}$ or $\frac{2}{4}$ from the Baroque Era (1600-1750).

171. GAVOTTE

J.S. Bach

Andante

Theory — Enharmonics

Enharmonics are two different note names which are both the same pitch.

(See page 47 for more examples.)

G♯ = A♭

172. ABA DABA

Theory — Chromatic Scale

A chromatic scale is made up of consecutive half steps. It is usually written with sharps (♯) going up and flats (♭) going down.

173. SLIDING CHROMATIC FINGERING

Remember the "natural" 1/2 steps: E-F and B-C

174. HABANERA

175. SHIFTING CHROMATIC FINGERING

176.

CHROMATICS

You can add beauty and feeling to your sound with VIBRATO, a smooth pulsation of the tone. It is created by varying the pitch slightly. Try these vibrato Work-outs as directed by your teacher.

1. The Slide
Place your second finger on the G string. Slide up and down the string, covering the distance of 3 half-steps, then 2 half-steps, and finally 1 half-step. Your thumb should slide with the hand. Try this motion while using long, sustained bow strokes.

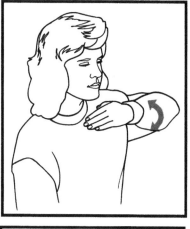

2. The Pivot
Touch the second finger of your left hand to your collarbone. Then pivot (rotate) your arm while keeping the elbow relatively still.

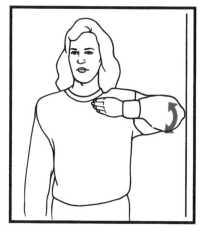

To check the motion away from the instrument, touch your elbow to the wall while doing The Pivot.

3. Pivot And Bow
Continue doing The Pivot motion, while playing long tones on open strings.

4. Vibrato
With your left thumb behind the neck, place your second finger on B♭ on the G string and vibrate while playing a long, sustained bow stroke. Continue with first finger on A, and finally with fourth finger on B.

Master these Work-outs before using VIBRATO in your playing!

VIBRATO EXERCISES

First practice these vibrato exercises without bowing. The lower part of the vibrato motion is shown in small notes, which do not denote actual pitches.

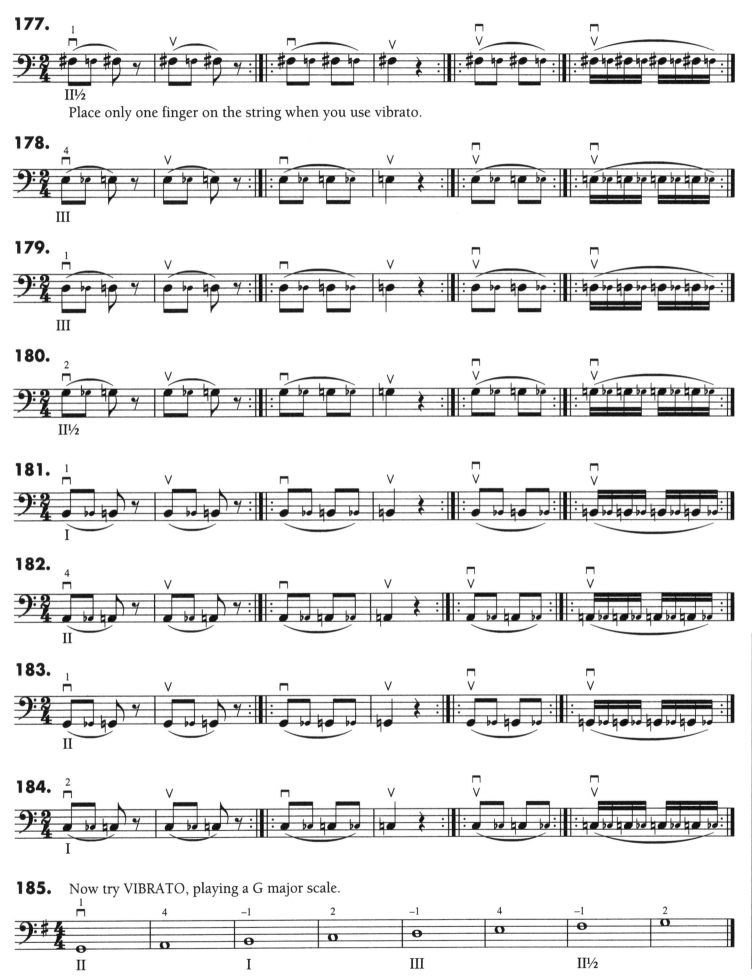

Place only one finger on the string when you use vibrato.

185. Now try VIBRATO, playing a G major scale.

MORE VIBRATO EXERCISES

186.

III

187.

III

188.

I

189.

III

190.

II

191.

II

192.

III

193.

I

194. Use VIBRATO.

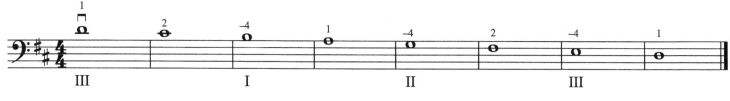

III   I   II   III

Spiccato Bowing   A light bouncing stroke in the lower half of the bow.

Play spiccato (off the string) or staccato (on the string) as directed by your teacher. Spiccato is normally used in medium and faster tempos.

Spiccato Notation:

195.

196.

197.

198.

199.

200.

201.

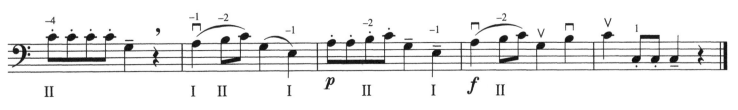

SPICCATO

Now try spiccato with two or more notes in the same direction.

202.

203.

204.

205.

206.

207.

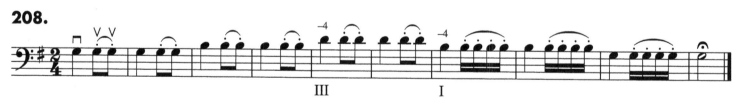

208.

209. **Allegretto**

Louré (Portato) Bowing — Long hooked notes. There is only a slight separation between notes.

Louré Notation:

210.

III

211.

212.

III   I   II½ III   II½

213. THEME FROM SYMPHONY NO. 7

Ludwig van Beethoven

Tremolo Bowing — Very fast, short strokes played in the upper half of the bow. Pull your bow faster and longer to start accented tremolo strokes.

Tremolo Notation:

214.

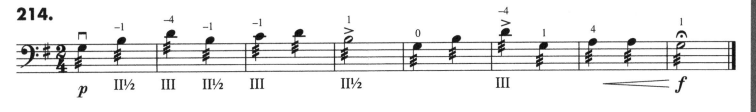

II½ III II½ III   II½   III

215. TAPS

II½ III II½

LOURÉ - TREMOLO

Special Notation

♩ = ♫

♩ = ♬

When a quarter note is written with a beam through it, it is played like two eighth notes. When a quarter note is written with two beams through it, it is played like four sixteenth notes.

216.

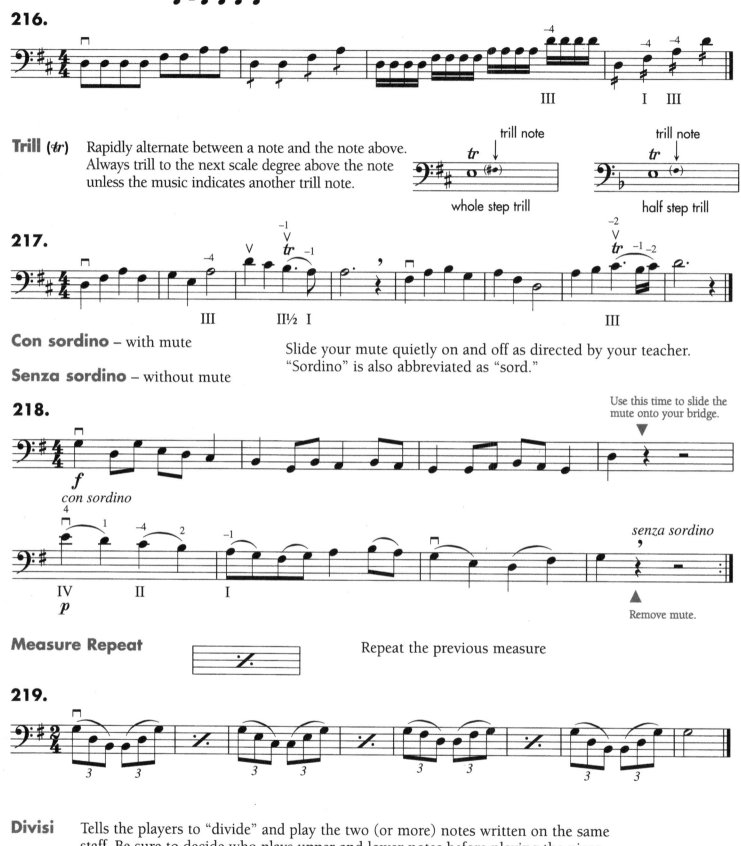

Trill (*tr*)

Rapidly alternate between a note and the note above. Always trill to the next scale degree above the note unless the music indicates another trill note.

whole step trill

half step trill

217.

Con sordino – with mute

Senza sordino – without mute

Slide your mute quietly on and off as directed by your teacher. "Sordino" is also abbreviated as "sord."

218.

Use this time to slide the mute onto your bridge.

con sordino

senza sordino

Remove mute.

Measure Repeat

Repeat the previous measure

219.

Divisi

Tells the players to "divide" and play the two (or more) notes written on the same staff. Be sure to decide who plays upper and lower notes before playing the piece. *Divisi* is usually abbreviated *div.* Unis., or unison, tells performers to play the same note.

220.

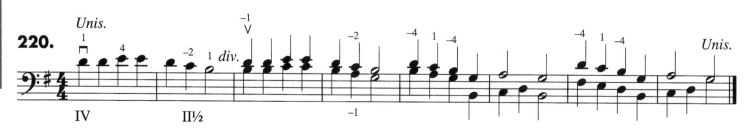

FOR DOUBLE BASSES ONLY

INTRODUCING TENOR CLEF

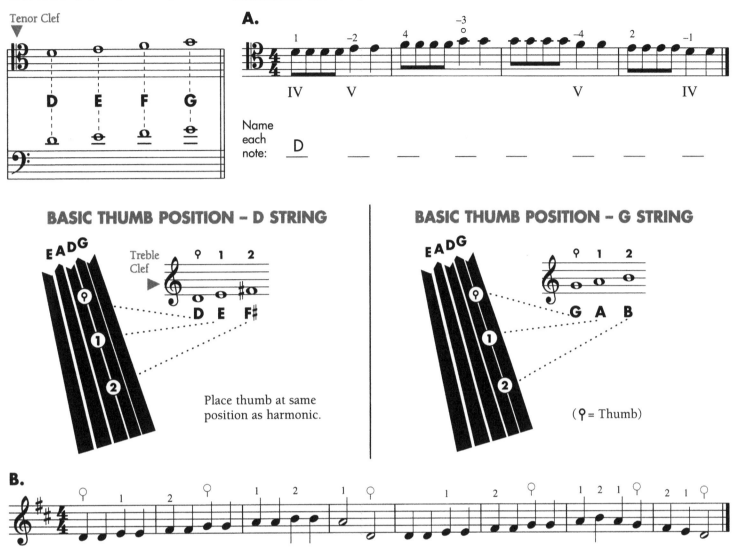

Tenor Clef

D E F G

A.

IV   V   V   IV

Name each note: D ___ ___ ___ ___ ___ ___

BASIC THUMB POSITION – D STRING

Treble Clef

D E F#

Place thumb at same position as harmonic.

BASIC THUMB POSITION – G STRING

G A B

(♀ = Thumb)

B.

JAZZ BASS LINES

Jazz bass lines are usually played pizzicato, and are often improvised. Important chord tones should be played on strong beats (such as 1 and 3). Add scale steps between them to create "passing tones" on weaker beats. For example:

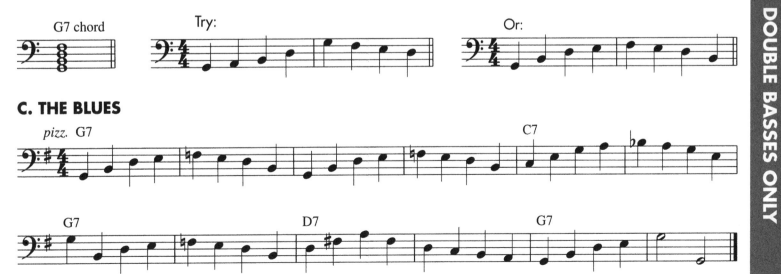

G7 chord   Try: Or:

C. THE BLUES

pizz. G7   C7

G7   D7   G7

DOUBLE BASS FINGERING CHART

Positions: ½ - I - II½ - III - IV - V - VI - Harmonics

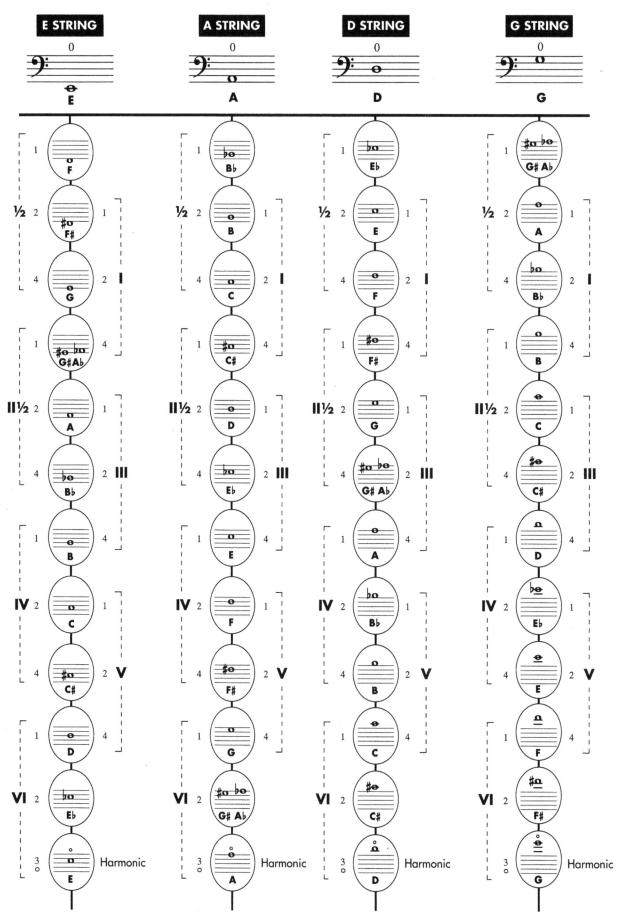

See page 45 for Thumb Position and Tenor Clef.

DOUBLE BASS FINGERING CHART

Positions: I - II - III½ - V½ - Harmonics

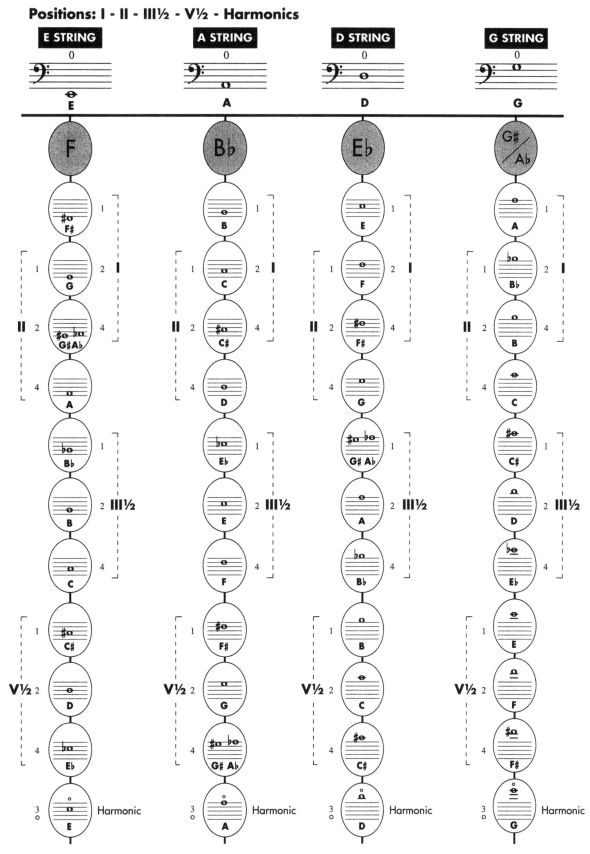

Enharmonics

All sharps and flats have enharmonics which are usually played at the same place on the string, but may be played by a different finger. For example, a G# on the D string is played by 2nd finger in 3rd position. The G# is at the same spot where A♭ is played by 1st finger in 3rd ½ position. Common enharmonics:

| C# Db | D# Eb | E Fb | E# F | F# Gb | G# Ab | A# Bb | B Cb | B# C |

FINGERING CHARTS

GLOSSARY and INDEX

Essential Element	Definition	Essential Element	Definition
Chromatic scale	A scale made up of consecutive half steps. (p. 37)	Portato	(*Louré*) Legato bowing style with long hooked notes (p. 43)
Con sordino	With mute. (p. 44)	Senza Sordino	Without mute. (p. 44)
Divisi	Divided upper and lower notes among players. (p.44)	Shifting	Slide left hand smoothly and lightly to new location on fingerboard.
Enharmonics	Two different letter names for the same pitch. (p. 37)		
Louré	(*Portato*) Legato bowing style with long hooked notes. (p. 43)	Spiccato	Light bouncing bow stroke. (p. 41)
		Tremolo	Very fast short strokes in the upper half of the bow. (p. 43)
Measure repeat sign	Repeat the previous measure. (p. 44)	Trill *tr*	Alternate rapidly with the half or whole step above. (p. 44)
Natural Harmonic	String divided in half by lightly touching mid-point. (p. 5)	Vibrato	Smooth pulsation of the tone. (p. 38)

RHYTHM AND BOWING PATTERNS

Use the following rhythms and bowings with scales as directed by your teacher. Permission to photocopy this page is given by the publisher so that you can place these examples beside any other page.